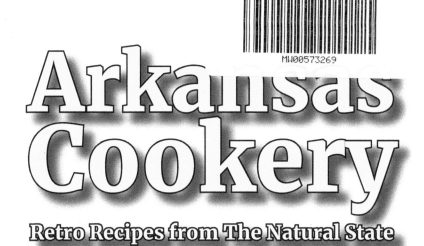

Arkansas Cookery

Retro Recipes from The Natural State

Arkansas Cookery

Retro Recipes from The Natural State

Kat Robinson

TONTI
PRESS

Published by Tonti Press
Little Rock, Arkansas
Copyright © 2021 by Kat Robinson. All rights reserved.

First published December 2021

Manufactured in the United States of America

ISBN: 978-1-952547-07-2

Library of Congress Control Number: 2021950462

EPUB release December 2021

ISBN: 978-1-952547-08-9

The author accepted no compensation for inclusion of any element in
this book. All photographs of food consist of edible, real food not en-
hanced with photographic tricks, manipulation or fakery. Photographs
were taken by the author on a Canon T7i camera with a 50mm
macro lens and a 17-40mm wide angle lens..

All photographs were taken on the property at The Writers' Colony
at Dairy Hollow in Eureka Springs, Arkansas. For information
about residencies, fellowships and the mission at the facility, please
visit WritersColony.org.

To Crescent Dragonwagon and Ned Shank
for the vision to share the delightful air of Eureka Springs
with a place for writers and artists to call home
and the joy that home has brought to hundreds who have found
artistic sanctuary at The Writers' Colony at Dairy Hollow.

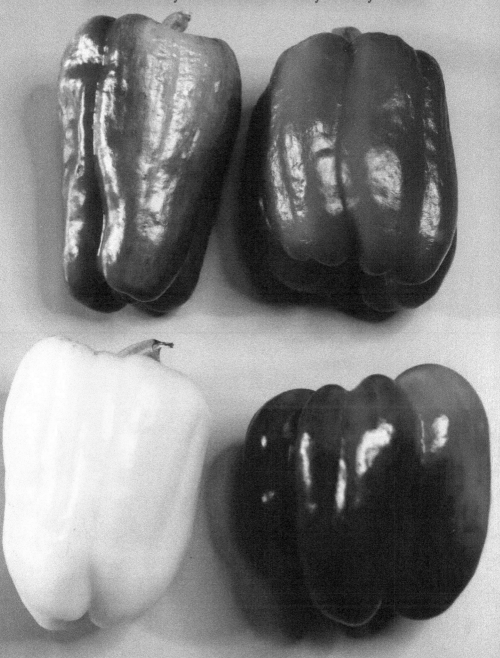

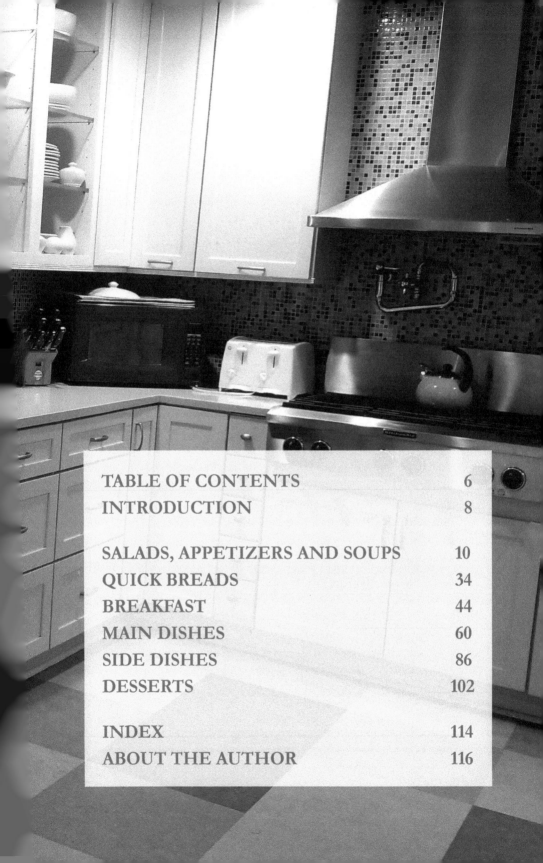

Four hundred cookbooks or more. Why? That's a complicated question.

I've been covering Arkansas food for years, first with its restaurants, then visiting farms and companies that make mixes and sauces, attending and even creating festivals and sitting down to record oral histories of our foodways. Along the way, I try to always stop in at the local bookstore, flea market or antique mall, searching for something as valuable as gold - local cookbooks.

Before the internet, our cooking tended to be somewhat regional, if not hyper local. Sure, we had Julia Child and Jacques Pepin, and a host of cookbooks ranging from high cuisine to TIME-LIFE's Foods of the World series. A cookbook could be gifted through family members and acquaintances, or picked up on a move from one part of the United States to another. But by and large, our food came from family traditions, working with our parents and grand-parents in the kitchen, and from recipes we found in our cookbooks.

The internet changed that. From its popularity blooming in the 1990s to the mass sharing on Facebook, how-tos from Tasty and quick step-by-steps on TikTok, our recipe pool is becoming more homogenized. Any search for cornbread on Google comes up with a selection of varieties that aren't so far apart. A generation that makes what it says on the back of the package when I was young now gets a quick recipe on the phone to read while measuring out those ingredients. Who's to say one version or another is the original any more?

Hence the cookbooks. In my efforts to try and document where our food came from, I gathered and hoarded every Arkansas cook-book I could find from the 20th Century, under the idea that these printed words would not change with time.

That's how I came to have 400 or so local cookbooks when the pandemic struck. When I sequestered myself in my mom's kitchen, reminiscing about times past and Zooming with my friends to see what they were making, I was pulling out those cookbooks, trying recipes, and marveling at how many spellings there were for a dish called Tallerine.

Friends such as Rebecca Lemley McGraw, Melanie Solomon, and Wendy Thibailt Kane came and brought books to my doorstep as I shared what I was doing. The stack grew. And one July day, when it looked like the pandemic had dwindled away, I took boxes of books and a whole car full of fresh local produce and such with me to Eureka Springs, where I took up residence for a couple of weeks in the Culinary Suite at The Writers' Colony at Dairy Hollow. It was in that fragment of time, between shooting and producing the *Arkansas Dairy Bars: Neat Eats and Cool Treats* film and actually bringing it to air, that I found myself digging into the recipes that now comprise this book.

Being back at Writers' Colony was good for my soul, a reminder that the world I'd withdrawn from in the worst of times was still right outside my window. I met and made friends of fellow writers in that small wedge of time when it felt safe to leave the mask in my pocket and enjoy evenings of Jana's cooking and the conversations of fellow writers.

Within this book, find the fruits of my labors, the many dishes that came out from trial and error, redactions and adjustments, a sampling of a wellspring of recipes preserved on paper. These dishes, which amused and fed several of my fellow writers, were conjured in the marvelous surroundings of a fully equipped kitchen made available during my residency, a wonderland of delights for anyone with the urge to try out some mad culinary skills.

My 400+ Arkansas cookbook collection continues to grow, and as I discover more delights within those pages, I plan to share more. For now, here's a sampler of culinary contributions to bring to your own table.

Kat Robinson
Little Rock
November 2021

3 egg whites
Pinch of salt
1 tsp. vanilla

SALADS
APPETIZERS
and SOUPS

Kat Robinson

FRUIT SALAD

Redacted from a recipe by Dorothy Lumbert, which appeared in *A Cookbook of Our Favorite Recipes* (1975) published for the Fort Smith Apple Blossom Chapter of the American Business Women's Association.

2 small cans mandarin oranges
1 15 ounce can pineapple chunks
7 ounces coconut flakes (1/2 bag)

5 ounces mini marshmallows
  (1.2 bag)
8 ounces sour cream

Drain oranges and pineapple chunks. Fold all ingredients together and allow to chill together for 3-4 hours before serving.

AMBROSIA SALAD

This is an amalgamated recipe adapted from six different cookbooks from the 1970s.

1 15 ounce can mandarin oranges
1 20 ounce can crushed pineapple
1 10 ounce can or bottle
  maraschino cherries
1 cup sweetened coconut

1 cup mini marshmallows
½ cup sour cream, room
  temperature
½ tub Cool Whip, completely
  thawed

Fold together Cool Whip and sour cream. Drain fruit. Fold all ingredients into cream mix. Cover tightly and refrigerate 3-4 hours before serving.

WALDORF SALAD

Common across the United States mid-century, this version by Melba Golden appears in *Talk About Good Cooks*, put together by the Southland Women's Club of Stuttgart.

1/3 cup mayonnaise	2 teaspoons lemon juice
Dash of salt	2 cups diced unpeeled red
2 cups diced celery	apples
1.2 cup coarsely chopped walnuts	lettuce leaves (optional)

In salad bowl, blend mayonnaise, lemon juice and salt. Add apples, celery and walnuts and toss well. Can serve on lettuce leaves.

QUICK APPLE-CELERY SALAD

Margaret Martin contributed this similar salad to the book *Umm Good* put together by the First United Methodist Women of North Little Rock, published in 1983.

3 or 4 medium apples, peeled and diced	1/4 to 3/8 cup mayonnaise
1 cup diced celery	1/4 cup broken walnut pieces
1/4 cup raisins	lettuce leaves

Mix apples, celery and raisins with mayonnaise. Place servings of salad on lettuce leaves. Sprinkle tops with broken nuts. Serves six.

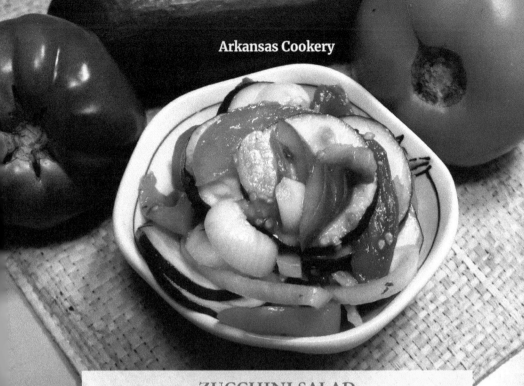

ZUCCHINI SALAD

This version was contributed by Betty Page to *Primrose Cooks* by the Primrose United Methodist Women of Little Rock.

2 zucchini, thinly sliced
2 tomatoes, cut into thin wedges
1 bell pepper, cut into thin rings

1 onion, sliced thinly and
   separated into rings
Oil and vinegar dressing

Combine vegetables and drizzle with dressing. Chill. Drain to serve.

ZUCCHINI SALAD

You'll find this version by Carol Brown in the 1984 *St. James Family Cookbook*, compiled by the Christian Mothers Fellowship at St. James United Methodist Church in Little Rock.

1/2 cup chopped green peppers
1/2 cup chopped celery
7 small zucchini, peeled and
   thinly sliced
3/4 cup sugar
1 teaspoon black pepper

1/3 cup oil
1/3 cup white vinegar
salt
Onions, sliced very thin
   (small green or sweet)

Combine all ingredients. Let stand. Can add halved cherry tomatoes if desired.

Kat Robinson

16

BLACK CHERRY SALAD

This recipe appears in several cookbooks in my collection. This version was redacted from *Favorite Recipes of the Women of Good shepherd* (1964) by The Episcopal Church of the Good Shepherd in Little Rock, contributed by Ella Mae Kidd.

1 can large black cherries
  or 1/2 pound fresh black cherries
1/4 cup pecans or almonds, whole
1 package lemon Jell-O

1 block cream cheese
1/2 pint whipping cream
2 Tablespoons confectioners
  sugar

Pit cherries and insert almond or pecan into each one. Add water to juice from cherries to make one pint; heat until boiling, then add Jell-O. Pack cherries into mold. When Jell-O begins to thicken, pour over cherries. Refrigerate to set.

Allow cream cheese to come to room temperature. Mash, then beat together with whipped cream and sugar. Spread in serving dish before unmolding. Can also be piled within circular molds.

ORANGE SALAD

Mrs. Paul Enderlin contributed the original recipe to *The King's Collection: Favorite Recipes of Christ The King Church* (1971, Little Rock).

1 large package
  Orange Jell-O
1 can crushed pineapple,
  drained, juice reserved

Water to add to juice
2 carrots, shredded
1/2 cup crushed nuts
  (pecans or walnuts)
lettuce leaves

Add juice to water to make 1 cup. Bring to boil. Add Jell-O mix, shredded carrots and crushed nuts. Add one cup cold water and immediately pour into mold. Refrigerate until firm. Unmold on bed of lettuce leaves.

STRAWBERRY SALAD

From Kelly Sanderson in *What's Cooking in 4-H* (1974).

2 packages strawberry Jell-O
2 cups hot water
1 package frozen strawberries

1 can undrained pineapple
3 bananas, mashed
1/2 pint sour cream

Mix Jell-O into hot water. Add strawberries, pineapple and banana. Pour half into greased mold and let set. Spread sour cream over layer, then add in remaining gelatin mix. Chill until firm.

17

several times during baki[...]

EN [...]

1/2 tsp. [...]
1/2 tsp. [...]

SODA CRACKER PIE

3 egg whites
Pinch of Salt
1 tsp. vanilla
[...]ker crumbs rolled fine (these must be

COCA-COLA SALAD

Congealed salads were a staple of luncheons and family gatherings in mid-century Arkansas, as they were across the United States. Many versions of this particular cherry cola salad can be found throughout our cookbooks from this period. This one is redacted from a version by Jewell Rickett from Gurdon High School, published in *Recipes from Arkansas* by the School Food Service Association in 1976.

1 can Coca-Cola
2 small boxes cherry Jell-O
1 10 ounce jar maraschino cherries
1 20 ounce can pineapple chunks

12 ounces (1 1.2 blocks) cream
    cheese, mashed
1 cup chopped nuts (pecans,
    walnuts or almonds)

Drain juice from pineapple and cherries and add water to equal 2 cups. Bring to a boil in saucepan. Add Jell-O and stir until dissolved. Remove from heat and add Coca-Cola, cherries, pineapple, cream cheese and nuts. Pour into mold. Refrigerate until firm.

TOMATO SOUP SALAD

Savory congealed salads were usually reserved for cocktail parties and afternoon gatherings. While there are fewer found in our cookbooks, they are present, particularly in post-World War II collections. This one comes from Auta Watson and appeared in *SCAT Cook's* by Senior Citizens Activities Today, Inc. in Little Rock.

1 can tomato soup
1 eight ounce block cream cheese
2 envelopes unflavored gelatin
1/2 cup cold water

1 cup mayonnaise
1/2 cup celery
1/2 cup chopped green pepper
1/2 cup finely chopped onion

Bring soup to boil. Add cream cheese. Stir until smooth. Dissolve gelatin in cold water. Add gelatin and mayonnaise to soup mixture. When cool, add remaining ingredients. Pour into greased mold. Chill until firm.

CHICKEN SALAD

This recipe appeared in *Family Recipe Collection* by the All Souls Church Ladies Aid of Scott, Arkansas, published in 1981 It says it makes enough for 20 small sandwiches, though the size isn't determined. I calculate it would make five sandwiches cut into quarters, which is how I suspect was what was originally intended. The other suggestion for service is to stuff the chicken salad in fresh tomatoes, as seen here, in which case the serving size depends on the size of the tomato.

In place of six chicken breasts, I substituted the meat of one whole chicken, roasted with just salt and pepper for seasoning. Taking the extra step to season the chicken brings a more complete flavor to the overall dish. Roasting the pecans amplifies the flavor, as does adding herbs or spices to the mayo before folding the ingredients together.

6 chicken breasts or one whole
    chicken, cooked and de-boned
1 medium apple, cored and diced
3/4 cup chopped celery
1 cup chopped pecans
Hellman's mayonnaise to taste

Suggested mayo add-ins:
Ground celery seed
Finely chopped tarragon
Finely chopped parsley
Salt and pepper

Dice chicken. Add other ingredients and mayo to taste. Let rest for at least one hour before serving. Makes five ample sandwiches or will fill 4-6 medium tomatoes.

STUFFED CUCUMBERS

This recipe comes from *Foods of Note* (1979) by the Fort Smith Symphony Orchestra.

2 medium cucumbers
6 ounces (3/4 block) cream cheese
2 Tablespoons onion, minced
2 Tablespoons bell pepper, minced

1.2 cup pecans, finely chopped
paprika to taste
Worcestershire to taste
Salt

Peel cucumbers; cut in half across cucumber. Scoop out inside and sprinkle with salt. Invert and let drain on paper towels in refrigerator two hours. With fresh paper towels, dry cucumbers.

Mix remaining ingredients and stuff cucumbers. Wrap tightly with plastic wrap and refrigerate overnight.

Slice in 1/4" sections across cucumber and serve immediately.

FRENCH TOMATO DELIGHT

Rita Wurtz submitted this recipe to *What's Happening in 4-H*, the 1976 cookbook from Pulaski County. This is for each serving.

1 medium fresh tomato   2-3 Tablespoons French dressing
1.2 cup cottage cheese   Dash of salt
1 Tablespoon minced bell pepper   Dash of pepper
1 Tablespoon minced green onion

Cut top off tomato and scoop out insides. Chop scooped tomato and mix into all other ingredients. Stuff back inside the tomato and serve. May top with shredded cheese.

MARINATED SALAD

Elwanda Bell of the Searcy Beethoven chapter of the Arkansas Federation of Music Clubs shared this recipe in *Musicians and the Culinary Arts* in 1984.

2 ripe avocados   1/4 cup Italian salad oil
3 ripe tomatoes

Slice avocados and quarter tomatoes. Mix together with oil. Other vegetables, such as cucumbers and squash can be added. Marinate several hours.

GREEN PEA SALAD

Mrs. Otto Elsass of Glaub Lone Holly gave this recipe to the Clay County Council of Home Demonstration Clubs for the book *Favorite Recipes from Clay County Kitchens*. This is from the second printing in 1955. I have to admit, I didn't think it looked all that great, but once I tried it, I was hooked - and enjoyed a couple of batches of this salad during my time at Writer's Colony.

1-15 ounce can of green or
   English peas, well drained
1 hard boiled egg, finely diced
1/2 cup celery, diced
1/2 teaspoon sugar

1/2 cup cream cheese, diced
1/2 cup nuts, diced fine
2 Tablespoons salad dressing
   (such as Miracle Whip)

Mix well. Let sit in the refrigerator one hour before serving.

THREE BEAN SALAD

A very popular side salad, found all across the state, even today, three bean salad is a sweet-and-sour delight that goes well with both cold and hot dishes. It's a great option as a lunchtime side and keeps well in the refrigerator for several days. This version of the recipe was submitted by several different school lunch ladies in the 1977 cookbook *Recipes from Arkansas* by the School Lunch Service Association.

1 can yellow wax beans, drained	1/2 cup vegetable oil
1 can kidney beans, drained	1/2 cup vinegar
1 can green beans, drained	3/4 cup sugar
1/2 cup chopped green bell peppers	1/4 teaspoon black pepper
1/2 cup finely chopped onion	1 teaspoon salt

Mix beans, green bell pepper and onion. Combine remaining ingredients and pour over vegetables. Cover and refrigerate overnight. Drain before serving. Makes six to eight servings.

SQUASH FRITTERS

Arkansas's climate is particularly good for growing all sorts of squash, from acorn to butternut, cushaw, patty-pan, yellow crook-necked to zucchini. Thanks to their proliferation in our gardens, there are so many ways we prepare them. This fried pattied squash can be made with any variety, but usually come from yellow squash to the table. This recipe is from the Arkansas Federation of Music Club's 1985 cookbook, *Musicians and the Culinary Arts*, submitted by Mary King of the Hope Friday Music Club.

2 cups grated raw squash	1/4 cup finely chopped onions
1 teaspoon salt	A dash of pepper
1 teaspoon sugar	1 egg, well beaten
1 Tablespoon flour	Oil for frying

Shake or sift together salt, sugar, flour and pepper. Fold together squash, onions and egg. Fold both mixtures together. Heat oil. Drop mixture by spoonfuls into hot oil. Turn when outside is brown. Remove to paper towel lined plate for draining. Serve hot.

A sauce for dipping: blend together 1/4 cup mayonnaise, 1/4 cup sour cream. 1 teaspoon Dijon or whole grain mustard, and 1/4 teaspoon each salt and pepper.

GUACAMOLE SALAD

The spread of nachos and cheese dip in cookbooks of the 1970s and 1980s parallels this delectable concoction's rise to appetizer delight. A good pairing with salsa for tortilla chip dipping, guacamole is now ubiquitous everywhere. This version is redacted from the Fort Smith Women in Construction *Book of Favorite Recipes* (1981) and is attributed to Brenda Love.

3 avocados, cubed
1/4 can Ro*Tel, drained and mashed
juice of 1/2 lemon
1/2 fresh tomato, chopped

1/2 green onion, chopped
1/4 teaspoon salt
dash of black pepper
dash garlic salt

Mix well and serve on lettuce leaves, or as a dip with tortilla chips.

SALSA

Becky Davidson contributed this recipe that appears in the 1982 Pike View Elementary School *Book of Favorite Recipes* (a common title of cookbooks printed by Circulation Service of Shawnee Hills, Kansas).

2 large tomatoes, chopped
1 bunch green onions, chopped
1 can black olives, drained and chopped
1 small can chopped green chilies

1 Tablespoon garlic salt
1 Tablespoon olive oil
1 Tablespoon vinegar

Mix all together. Let set in refrigerator 3-4 hours before serving.

LAYERED TACO DIP

Tortilla chips are credited to Rebecca Webb Carranza, a Los Angeles delicatessen owner who in 1940 started cutting up and frying wedges from misshapen tortillas that came from the restaurant's on-site automatic tortilla machine. They became a popular snack. Taco chips, on the other hand, were a flavored chip introduced by Doritos in 1967. Either chip can be used in Joyce Loughrige's recipe from *Arkansas Favorites*, published by the Arkansas Chapter of the Association of Legal Administrators. The chips seen here are from Maria's Tortilla Factory in Bentonville.

2 cans bean dip
1 can picante dip
1 12 ounce tub sour cream
3.4 head lettuce, chopped

3 tomatoes, chopped
1 onion, chopped
3/4 pound grated
      cheddar cheese

Bottom layer: bean dip, picante dip, sour cream. Top layer: lettuce, onion, tomatoes, cheese. Serve with taco chips.

HAM AND CHEESE BALL

This creation, which we call Ham Ball around our place, can actually be made with any thin-sliced smoked meat, whether it's ham, turkey ham, pastrami or even roast beef. Those little single-sandwich packets of ultra-thin sliced lunchmeat work well here; alternately, you can hand-slice or even chunk the meat, if you so choose. It appears in mostly the same ratios in 29 of my cookbooks, dating from 1964 to 1985.

2 eight ounce packages cream
   cheese, room temperature
8 ounces thinly sliced ham,
   turkey ham, or pastrami
1 bunch green onions, chopped
2 tablespoons diced pimento

1 teaspoon garlic salt
1/4 teaspoon salt
1/8 teaspoon black pepper
1/2 cup chopped pecans
   (optional) *or*
1 Tablespoon paprika (optional)

Combine all ingredients except pecans, folding together until consistency is same throughout. Shape into a ball. Roll in pecans or paprika and set on serving plate. Refrigerate until ready to serve.

CHICKEN CHUTNEY CHEESE BALL

Dorothy Rhodes submitted this recipe for *RX: Prepare As Directed and Enjoy!*, the 1977 cookbook of the Baptist Medical Center Arkansas Rehabilitation Institute Auxiliary.

1 cup cooked chicken
1 eight ounce block cream cheese
3/4 cups almonds, chopped
   and toasted

1/2 cup mayonnaise
2 Tablespoons chutney
1 Tablespoon curry powder
1 bunch parsley, chopped

Combine all ingredients except chicken, mixing well. Stir in chicken. Form into ball and wrap with plastic wrap. Chill at least six hours or overnight. Roll in parsley and return to refrigerator until ready to serve.

SHRIMP DIP

Diane Wheeler contributed this recipe to *Talk About Good Cooks!* by the Southland Women's Club of Stuttgart.

1 can cream of shrimp soup
8 ounce block cream cheese
2 drops lemon juice
   dash garlic salt
   dash paprika

Combine all ingredients and beat until creamy. Store in airtight container. Best if sets overnight.

```
SALMON CROQUETTES

1 one lb. can red salmon          1/4 cup cracker crumbs
1 egg, beaten                     1/2 tsp. salt
1/2 tsp. salt                     1/2 cup mashed potatoes
1/2 cup sweet milk                1 tsp. lemon juice
pepper to taste

Flake the  salmon; mix ingredients and form into croquettes.  Dip
in beaten egg, then roll in cracker crumbs.  Fry in deep fat.

Auta Watson                                               106
```

SALMON CROQUETTES

My mom has told me of the inflicted horrors of carp cakes, a dish of (sometimes home canned) carp beaten together with egg and crackers fried in a skillet and served at the table. From what I have gathered, it is a family delicacy on my father's side.

These are blessedly not those. This version utilizing salmon is attributed to Auta Watson and appears in *SCAT Cook's*, a cookbook published by Senior Citizens Activity Today, Inc., representing residents of three locations: Farris Tower Center on Broadway, Cumberland Towers Center on East Eighth Street, and Powell Towers Center on Wolfe Street. The original recipe is above - my redacted recipe is as follows.

1 pound fresh salmon   1 egg
1 teaspoon lemon juice   1/2 cup milk
1/2 teaspoon salt   1/2 cup saltine cracker crumbs
dash black pepper   1/2 cup mashed potatoes
Oil for cooking

Mix lemon juice, salt and pepper. Pour over salmon. Saute or bake salmon until done. Remove from heat, remove skin and flake.

Beat together egg and milk, then fold in crumbs and potatoes. Fold in salmon.

Bring oil to medium high heat in skillet. Form mixture into 1 inch balls and drop into hot oil. Press lightly with spatula. Turn once when browned. Remove to paper towel lined plate. Serve hot or cold.

To use smoked salmon in this recipe: do not cook salmon or add lemon juice, pepper or salt. Use 1/2 pound smoked salmon instead of one pound fresh salmon. Flake smoked salmon, then add to egg-milk-cracker-potato mixture and cook as directed.

31

COWBOY SOUP

A hearty and tasty stew best served with cornbread, this recipe comes from Birdye Farmer and appears in the 1984 *Our Best To You* cookbook by the Park Hill Christian Church of North Little Rock.

1 Tablespoon shortening or oil
1 pound lean ground beef
1 cup chopped onion
1 cup shredded cabbage
1 cup sliced carrots
1 cup sliced celery
2-16 ounce cans diced tomatoes

1 can corn, drained
 or 1 1/2 cup corn off the cob
4 cups water
1 teaspoon Cavender's Greek
 Seasoning
salt and pepper to taste

Brown beef and onion in oil in Dutch oven. Add all other ingredients, mix and bring to boil. Cover, reduce heat and simmer 1-2 hours. A good afternoon soup to leave bubbling on the back of the stove for those coming in on their own schedule.

CHICKEN AND DUMPLINGS

Most home chefs have their own version of this classic. In fact, it wasn't easy to find even a basic recipe for the dish. This version comes from Jerry Alexander and was published in *Delights from the Delta II* by the Chicot County 4-H & Extension Homemakers Clubs.

4 chicken breasts	2 sticks oleo or butter
2 cups flour	Chopped celery, onion, carrots,
7 Tablespoons Crisco	up to 3/4 cup *optional*
3 3/4 cups milk	Herbs if desired

Cook breasts in eight cups water and one stick oleo or butter until tender. Remove chicken from broth, de-bone and return to broth.

Mix together flour and Crisco. Add 3/4 cup milk to make dough. Knead and roll on floured surface to desired thickness. Cut into strips.

Add remaining milk and oleo or butter to broth and bring to boil. Drop dumplings in and add salt and pepper to taste. Stir often and cook on low heat for 20 minutes.

If desired, you may add chopped celery, onion and/or carrots along with choice of herbs (up to 3/4 cup total) to broth while boiling chicken.

QUICK BREADS

Kat Robinson

36

BANANA NUT BREAD

There are so many versions of banana nut bread out there (including my sour cream and brown sugar version) that leaving it out of this book was unconscionable. This recipe by Tanya Fikes of Montgomery County appeared in the 1981 Arkansas Farm Bureau Federation Women's Committee's *Arkansas Farm Favorites* cookbook.

1/2 cup butter	2 cups flour
1/2 cup sugar	1/2 teaspoon baking powder
2 eggs	1/2 teaspoon baking soda
1 1/2 cups mashed banana	1/2 teaspoon salt
1/2 cup chopped nuts	

Cream butter in mixing bowl; gradually add sugar and beat until light and fluffy. Beat in eggs one at a time. Blend in bananas and nuts. Sift together dry ingredients. Gradually add to creamed mixture, beating only until blended. Pour into loaf pan. Bake at 350°F for 40-50 minutes. Cool in pan on wire rack for 10 minutes turn out of pan and continue to cool on wire rack.

PUMPKIN BREAD

Not to be confused with pumpkin roll, which is similar but a roll cake with a cream cheese filling, this moist recipe works for both loaves and muffins. Polly Gray with the Jonesboro Promenaders submitted this recipe to the cookbook *Culinary Classics of the Arkansas State Square Dance Federation*.

1-16 ounce can pumpkin	1 1/2 teaspoons soda
3 eggs	1 1/4 cup teaspoons salt
3/4 cup oil	3/4 teaspoon nutmeg
1/2 cup water	3/4 teaspoon cinnamon
2 1/2 cups flour	1/2 cup raisins
2 1/4 cups sugar	1/2 cup chopped pecans

Beat eggs, pumpkin, oil and water together. Stir together flour, sugar, soda, salt, nutmeg, and cinnamon. Fold into egg mixture. Add raisins and pecans. Bake at preheated 350°F oven for 1 hour 15 minutes in two greased 9x5 inch loaf pans. Test in center with toothpick. If not done, bake five minutes more each time then test again.

DATE NUT BREAD

This bread is so good, it could have cost a fight. I brought it down to Jana's kitchen in the common area at Writer's Colony to share with the rest of the writers in residence. I also made a second loaf for myself - but when it went over so well, I went ahead and shared that loaf with the crew, too. And yes, I ended up making another loaf to enjoy the rest of my stay, even though I was surrounded by tasty food. It's absolutely magnificent.

This recipe by Mrs. Jewell Teeter appeared in a cookbook put together by the Women's Society of Christian Service at Asbury Methodist Church in Little Rock in 1954. It has a lovely chocolate note to it and was just as good in July as it would be in December.

This is one sweet quick bread you'll certainly love to serve with milk or coffee. I recommend lightly toasting your slices with a small pat of butter for maximum enjoyment.

1 1/2 cups margarine or butter

2 cups boiling water

2 teaspoons soda

1 cup chopped nuts
  walnuts recommended

1 cup pitted and chopped dates

1 cup brown sugar, packed

1 cup granulated sugar

2 eggs

1 teaspoon vanilla

4 cups sifted flour

Stir soda, nuts and dates into boiling water (the concoction may turn black - don't worry, it's a chemical reaction between the nuts and the soda). Cook four minutes, stirring constantly. Cool.

Cream together margarine and sugars. Add eggs and vanilla and beat until fluffy. Fold in flour and the date mixture. Mix well.

Heat oven to 325°F. Grease two 9x5 loaf plans. Pour in batter.

Bake an hour and 15 minutes and test for doneness; if not done, bake an additional 15 minutes. Remove to wire rack for cooling.

To store: Wrap in foil or heavy wax paper and keep in deep freeze. Will keep indefinitely.

ZUCCHINI BREAD

Sylvia Lamb's version of this ever-popular favorite appears in the 1979 cookbook *Feasting on God's Goodness* from the Chastain Chapel General Baptist Church in Tumbling Shoals.

3 eggs	1 cup oil
2 cups sugar	2 cups grated zucchini
1 cup chopped nuts	2 cups flour
1/4 teaspoon baking soda	1 teaspoon salt
3 teaspoons cinnamon	3 teaspoons vanilla

Beat eggs until fluffy. Add oil, sugar and zucchini. Sift in dry ingredients. Add vanilla and nuts. Mix and pour into two greased 9x5 loaf pans. Bake at 350°F for one hour and 15 minutes.

MOLASSES BREAD

This recipe from Connie Davis comes from *Kissin' Wears Out, Cookin' Don't*, a 1977 cookbook by the Baptist Young Women of Levy Baptist Church in North Little Rock

2 1/4 cups flour	1 cup molasses
1 teaspoon salt	1 egg
1 teaspoon baking soda	1 cup applesauce
1 teaspoon cinnamon	1 cup (total) chopped raisins,
1/2 cup soft shortening	nuts or dried fruits

Combine dry ingredients. Cut in shortening or butter. Add molasses, egg, and applesauce. Beat well. Add raisins, dried fruits and./or nuts. Put in greased and floured loaf or cake pan and bake at 350°F for an hour, until a toothpick inserted in the middle comes out clean. If it browns too quickly, turn down the temperature.

CORNBREAD

This basic cornbread recipe is heavy on cornmeal and light on flour, making for a heavier, crumblier bread good for eating with greens and stews. It comes from Youlanda Miller and appeared in the 1977 cookbook *Red Hot Cookin'*, put together by the Almyra Fire Department Auxiliary. The cornbread in this photo was made with all-organic blue cornmeal from War Eagle Mill near Rogers.

1 1/2 cup cornmeal
3 tablespoons flour
1 teaspoon soda
1 teaspoon salt

2 cups buttermilk
1 egg
2 Tablespoons Wesson oil

Sift dry ingredients into bowl. Add buttermilk and egg, stirring until combined. Add oil to batter. Pour into hot, greased pan and bake at 450°F for 20-25 minutes.

CORNBREAD

The debate between whether or not cornbread should be sweet or not has been with us for ages. Sweetened cornbread in general tends to be more prevalent in the northern United States, where flour to cornmeal ratios are more even and cornbread can reach a more muffin-like consistency.

This version comes from Pat Greer and appears in *A Lovin' Spoonful*, a 1975 cookbook by the Levy United Methodist Church.

1 1/2 cup yellow cornmeal	2 Tablespoons baking powder
1/2 cup sifted flour	2 eggs, beaten
1/4 cup sugar	1 1/4 cup milk
1 teaspoon salt	3 Tablespoons melted
3/4 teaspoons baking soda	shortening

Sift dry ingredients together. In separate bow, combine eggs, milk and shortening. Add dry ingredients all at once and stir lightly. Bake at 425°F for 20-25 minutes.

43

BREAK
FAST

BREAKFAST CASSEROLE

One of the more splendid cookbooks in my collection is *Old World Cookery: Italian and European Favorites* by the Our Lady of the Lake Altar Society in Lake Village. It's an excellent repository of tasty dishes from Italy, marinated in the beauty of the Arkansas Delta. This particular casserole comes from the kitchen of Leslie C. Borgognoni.

1 pound sausage	6 eggs
4 slices bread	2 cups half-and-half
1 1/2 cups shredded sharp Cheddar	1 teaspoon salt
	1 teaspoon dry mustard

Crumble sausage in a skillet. Cook over medium heat until brown; drain well.

Cut bread into 1/2 inch cubes and spread in the bottom of a buttered baking dish. Top with sausage and cheese.

Combine eggs, half-and-half and seasonings. Beat well and pour over cheese. Cover and refrigerate overnight.

Heat oven to 350°F. Bake for 30 to 40 minutes until set. Yields 6 to 8 servings.

BAKED EGGS AND CHEESE SOUFFLE

Mrs. Winans Thompson submitted this recipe to the 1973 cookbook *Our Daily Bread*, compiled by The Morton-Wayland Group, United Methodist Women of First United Methodist Church in North Little Rock.

4 slices bread	5 eggs
2 Tablespoons butter	1 cup milk
1 1/2 cups shredded cheese	salt to taste

Butter bread and place in baking pan, buttered side down. Sprinkle shredded cheese over bread.

Beat eggs and add milk and salt to taste. Pour over bread and cheese. Cover with foil and refrigerate 12-24 hours.

Heat oven to 325°F. Bake for 45 minutes, removing foil during last few minutes of baking.

ONION-RICE OMELET

Mrs. Walton T. Champion's recipe appears in the 1952 cookbook *Kitchen Capers*, from The Riceland Garden Club Members of Stuttgart.

2 or 3 green onions, chopped	2 eggs
2 Tablespoons cooked rice	Dash of salt
2 Tablespoons milk or cream	Dash of pepper

Place onions and rice in a heated, greased frying pan. Brown and place in small dish. Beat whole eggs until fluffy. Beat in one tablespoon milk or cream for each egg. Add salt and pepper.

Pour into hot greased skillet and cook over low heat. When under-surface becomes set, start lifting edge with spatula to let uncooked part flow underneath. When omelet is cooked, sprinkle surface with fried rice and onions. Fold omelet and serve immediately

TOMATO FRITATTA

Another recipe from *Old World Cookery: Italian and European Favorites* by the Our Lady of the Lake Altar Society; this is from Regetta Mazzanti.

1 Tablespoon butter	1/2 teaspoon oregano
1/4 cup chopped onion	Salt and pepper to taste
8 eggs	1 large tomato, seeded and
2 Tablespoons grated Parmesan	chopped

In large oven-proof skillet, melt butter. Add onion and cook over medium heat until soft. Beat together the eggs, cheese, oregano, salt and pepper until well-blended. Pour over oven in skillet. Cook just until eggs are beginning to set at edges. Sprinkle tomato over egg mixture. Cook until eggs are set, 4 to 6 minutes longer. Broil about six inches from heat until light brown., 2 to 3 minutes. Very good.

Most home cooks of the era just knew how to make biscuits; like our historical forbearers, there are just some recipes you learn in your mother's kitchen that rarely need written down. Fortunately for future generations, some recipes are preserved in text. These three biscuit recipe are from *Come Into The Kitchen*, assembled by the Women's Society of Christian Service with Russellville's First United Methodist Church. These are from the book's second printing in 1965.

BISCUITS

This unattributed recipe is the first in the book.

2 cups flour	1/2 cup shortening
1 teaspoon baking powder	12/3 cup milk
1 teaspoon salt	

Sift first three ingredients together, then cut in shortening. Stir in milk until the dough sticks together. Roll and cut into biscuits. Bake at 425°F 12 to 15 minutes.

PARTY BISCUITS

Mrs. Howard Malone contributed this appetizer-style recipe.

2 cups flour	1/2 teaspoon cream of tartar
1/2 teaspoon salt	4 teaspoons baking powder
1 teaspoon sugar	1/2 cup shortening
2/3 cup milk or cream	

Sift dry ingredients, cut in shortening, knead very gently. Roll 1/4 inch thick. Use small biscuit cutter. Brush tops with milk or cream. Bake in hot oven (425°F. to 455°F) 8-10 minutes.

YEAST BISCUITS

Mrs. G.M. Cook submitted this recipe fro Louise Pramburger.

1 block cake yeast	1 heaping teaspoon baking
2 cups flour	powder
1 cup buttermilk	1 level Tablespoon sugar
1/2 cup shortening	1 teaspoon salt
1/2 teaspoon soda	1/4 cup lukewarm water.

Dissolve yeast in water. Add dry ingredients. Work shortening into flour and add to mixture gradually. Let rise one half hour. Bake in moderate oven.

CHERRY PRESERVES

When you can find them, cherries are a real treasure here. Birds tend to et most of our fruit, but if you manage to save a couple of pounds, this recipe will help you put them up right.

2 pounds pitted cherries   3 1/4 cups sugar
1 3.5 ounce box pectin   1/2 Tablespoon butter

Heat cherries, pectin, butter and 1/4 cup sugar over high flame in a Dutch oven until the mixture reaches a high boil. Add remaining sugar, boil an additional minute, stirring constantly. Remove from heat and skim foam off the top. Spoon preserves into hot sterilized jars to 1/4 inch from top. Put on lids and screw on rings to fingertip tight. Boil jars 10 minutes, then remove from heat and let counter cool for 24 hours before storing.

UNCOOKED STRAWBERRY PRESERVES

This recipe comes from *Our Daily Bread* (1971) from the North Little Rock First United Methodist Church Morton-Wayland Group.

3 cups fresh mashed strawberries   3/4 cups water
4 1/2 cups sugar   1 package Sure Jell

Stir strawberries and sugar together well, then let sit 30 minutes, stirring occasionally.

Bring water and Sure Jell to a boil for one minute, stirring well. Pour into strawberry mixture and stir until thickened. Pour into jars. Let set 23 hours, then store in refrigerator or freezer. Great with ice cream.

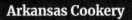

SAUSAGE CREAM GRAVY ON BISCUITS

All good Southern cooks know how to make biscuits and gravy... eventually. But for a crowd? This oversized recipe serves 50. It appears in the Pine Bluff Neighbor to Neighbor program's *Feeding Your Neighbor* cookbook.

4 pounds breakfast sausage   5 pounds biscuit mix
3 cups flour   Water for biscuit mix
6 quarts milk, heated and still hot

Crumble and fry sausage in a Dutch oven until barely done but not hard. Do not drain. Stir flour into sausage and grease. Add hot milk gradually, stirring constantly. Continue to cook until gravy has thickened, 15-20 minutes.

Prepare biscuit mix as directed. Spread over 1 commercial sheet pan or four cookie sheets. Score into 100 portions. Bake as directed. One serving = two biscuits plus 1/3 cup sausage cream gravy.

BLUEBERRY MUFFINS

This scone-like version of muffins comes from a recipe by Carol Koonce in the 1980 *Whiteville Missionary Baptist Church Ladies Auxiliary Cookbook* from Pine Bluff.

3 cups sifted flour
4 teaspoons baking powder
1/2 cup sugar
1/2 teaspoon salt

1 cup frozen or canned
  blueberries, well drained
2 eggs, beaten
1/4 cup oil
1 cup milk

Sift dry ingredients together. Mix in blueberries. Add eggs, oil, and milk, stirring just enough to dampen. Fill greased muffin tins 2/3 full. Bake at 400°F for 20 minutes. Yields 15 to 20 muffins.

SIX WEEK BRAN MUFFINS

Sometimes the best recipes are those tucked into old cookbooks. I found this tucked into a cookbook once owned by Pat Lemley.

2 cups boiling water
2 cups Nabisco 100% Bran Cereal
5 cups flour
5 Tablespoons soda
1 heaping cup shortening

3 1/2 cups sugar
4 eggs
4 cups Kellogg's All Bran
1 quart buttermilk

Mix Bran Cereal into boiling water. Set aside. Sift together flour and soda and mix into cereal. Cream shortening and sugar together, then add four eggs, one at a time. Bring all ingredients together. Bake for 15 minutes at 375°F. Can be kept in refrigerator for up to six weeks.

6 weeks Bran Muffins

2 cups Boiling Water — mix
2 cups Nabisco 100% Bran Cereal — set aside
Sift 5 cups Flour - 5 tab soda (mix together)
1 heaping cup shortening - 3½ cups sugar
4 eggs (one at a time)
4 cup Kellogg - all Bran -
1 qt. Buttermilk — combine togather
Bake 15 min. 375°
Will keep 6 weeks in refrigerate

SPINACH QUICHE

This strangely egg-free version of the popular breakfast dish is actually quite good, even if misnamed. It was submitted to the 1977 cookbook *RX Prepare as Directed and Enjoy* by the Baptist Medical Center Arkansas Rehabilitation Institute Auxiliary by Evelyn Ward.

1 unbaked pie crust	1-4 ounce can mushrooms
1 small onion, diced	3/4 pound Swiss or Feta cheese
2 Tablespoons butter or oleo	2 packages frozen spinach

Saute onion in butter. Add mushrooms, cheese and spinach. Fold into unbaked pie crust. Bake at 350°F for an hour.

QUICHE LORRAINE

This bacon-and-cheese quiche is attributed to Harold Thompson and appears in the 1977 *Dash of This, Pinch of That Cookbook* assembled by the United Methodist Women of First United Methodist Church of Conway.

1 unbaked pie crust	1 1/2 cups cream or half-and-half
6 slices cooked, crumbled bacon	1/2 teaspoon salt
8 ounces Swiss cheese, grated	1/8 teaspoon pepper
3 large eggs	1 Tablespoon butter

Sprinkle bacon and cheese over pie crust. Beat the eggs together with the cream, salt and pepper, then pour over cheese in pie crust. Break butter into small places and drop onto filling. Bake at 375°F for 35-40 minutes or until an inserted knife comes out clean. Let cool 10 minutes before serving.

ORANGE MUFFINS

St. Paul's United Methodist Church in Little Rock shared its 85th Anniversary cookbook in 1995, including recipes from decades of cooks. This 1970 recipe was submitted by Betty Compton.

1/2 cup butter	1 cup sugar
2 eggs	2 cups flour
1 teaspoon soda dissolved in	1 teaspoon vanilla
1 cup buttermilk	Juice of two oranges
Grated rind of two oranges	1/2 cup sugar

Mix first eight ingredients together and bake in muffin tins at 375°F for 15 minutes. Let cool 10 minutes. Mix remaining two ingredients and bring to boil. Pour over prepared muffins.

OLD FASHION BREAD PUDDING

Made with biscuits instead of bread, this is a good way to use up extra biscuits at the end of the day - as if that was ever such a thing. This recipe comes from Carolyn Ashmead and appears in *Our Favorite Recipes* from the Sheridan Athletic Boosters. I am assuming from the directions that the biscuits in question are the large ones we call "cathead biscuits" - biscuits the size of a cat's head.

3 baked biscuits, crumbled	1 cup sugar
2 cups milk	1/4 cup melted butter
4 eggs, well beaten	1 teaspoon vanilla

Combine all ingredients and stir well. Pour into 1 1/2 quart casserole. Pour 1/2 inch of water in baking pan. Place casserole in pan of water. Bake at 350°F for one hour.

OZARK BREAD PUDDING

Out of the same cookbook, you'll find this more traditional version shared by Virginia Smith.

7 cups stale bread crumbs	1 teaspoon cinnamon
3 eggs	1 teaspoon vanilla
1 1/2 cup half-and-half, scalded	3 Tablespoons butter
1/2 cup raisins	1 1/2 cup brown sugar

Toss bread crumbs with raisins and cinnamon. Combine eggs and half-and-half and vanilla. Pour over bread mixture and allow to soak for 10 minutes. Pour into a buttered 9x9 baking dish. Dot with butter. Bake in a preheated 325°F oven for one hour.

FIVE MINUTE COFFEE CAKE

Rusty Nelson submitted this to *Cook's Delight*, put together by the Victory Baptist Elementary Parent Teacher Fellowship in 1970.

3/4 cups sugar	3 teaspoons baking powder
1/2 cup shortening	1/2 teaspoon salt
2 eggs	1 teaspoon vanilla
1/2 cup milk	1/2 cup cinnamon and sugar
1 3/4 cups flour	mixture

Cream shortening and sugar. Add eggs and vanilla. Mix well. Add sifted dry ingredients alternately with the milk. Sprinkle cinnamon and sugar mixture over top. Spread in prepared 9 inch square pan. Bake at 350°F for 25-30 minutes. Serve warm. May be reheated.

MAIN DISHES

BEEF AND MUSHROOMS

This recipe is similar to the beef stroganoff, but doesn't include the sour cream present in most stroganoffs.

1 pound beef (sirloin or roast)
4 Tablespoons butter 1 large onion, diced
1 can mushrooms, drained
1 garlic clove, minced

2 Tablespoons flour
1 Tablespoon tomato paste
1 can beef broth
Salt and pepper to taste

Cut beef into one inch cubes. Saute in skillet, set aside. Add butter to pan, then saute mushrooms, garlic and onion until onion is translucent. Remove vegetables. Add flour to butter in pan, and stir until it thickens. Add all other items and bring to medium heat. Add one cup water, reduce heat and let simmer 1-2 hours.

BEEF STROGANOFF (TRADITIONAL)

This version by Mrs. William H. Riley comes from the 1971 *The King's Collection: Favorite Recipes from Christ The King Church*, in Little Rock.

2 pounds sirloin steak,
    cut into strips
1/4 cup flour
dash pepper
1-4 ounce can sliced mushrooms

1/4 cup butter
1/2 cup chopped onions
1 garlic clove, minced
1 cup beef broth
1 cup sour cream

Dust sirloin with flour and pepper. Brown meat in butter. Add mushrooms, onions and garlic and brown lightly. Stir in broth, cover and cool one hour, or until meat is tender. Gradually stir in sour cream over low heat five minutes.

BEEF STROGANOFF

This version comes from the 1976 *Recipes from Arkansas* cookbook published by the School Food Service Association Like many versions in Arkansas cookbooks, this one includes tomato soup. Ketchup is also often included in the dish, even though no tomatoes of any sort are in the original European recipe.

1 pound round steak	1 stick butter
or ground beef	1 large onion
1 Tablespoon dry mustard	1 can mushrooms with liquid
3 Tablespoons flour	1 can tomato soup
1 1/2 teaspoons salt	1.2 soup can water
1/4 teaspoon pepper	1/2 cup sour cream

Trim fat from meat. Cut meat into 1/2 inch x 1 1/2 inch strips. Sprinkle mustard, flour, salt and pepper over meat and mix well. Set aside for 15 minutes. Using half of butter, fry meat over fast fire until well browned. Fry separately in remaining butter, thinly sliced onion and mushrooms. Mix all together in large skillet. Add tomato soup, liquid reserved from mushrooms and water. Cover and simmer over low heat for two hours. About 15 minutes before serving, add sour cream. Serve over rice.

CABBAGE ROLLS

Marilyn Smith provided this recipe for the once-popular entree served with the baked potatoes that hold the rolls together. It appears in the Sheridan Athletics Booster cookbook *Our Favorite Recipes*.

1 pound ground beef
1 1/2 cups cooked rice
1 small diced onion
1 large head of cabbage

2 eggs
1 large can tomatoes *optional*
salt and pepper to taste
several large potatoes, peeled

Mix ground beef, rice, onions and eggs. Core cabbage head and break away outer leaves. Wash cabbage leaves and let stand a few minutes in warm water, until leaves begin to wilt. On each leaf, place two tablespoons of the beef mixture. Fold sides of leaf in over beef and roll it from bottom to top end, then secure with a toothpick. Place "seam" side down in baking pan. Repeat with remaining filling and leaves. Cut potatoes in half and lay across cabbage rolls. Mix tomatoes in their juice (if using) with salt, pepper and enough water to make a broth to submerge the rolls. Pour over. Cover and cook at 350°F for 35-40 minutes or until cabbage is tender.

BEEF GOULASH

This 1970 recipe from Karen Smith appears in the Victory Baptist Elementary cookbook *Cook's Delight*.

1/3 cup chopped onions	1 cup water
1 medium bell pepper	1/2 teaspoon salt
4 Tablespoons fat or butter	1 teaspoon black pepper
1 pound ground beef	1 1/2 Tablespoon chili powder
1-8 ounce can tomato sauce	1 1/2 cup uncooked pasta

Cook onions and pepper in hot fat until translucent. Add meat. Brown lightly. Add tomato sauce, water and seasoning. Simmer 30-40 minutes. Boil the pasta in salted water. Drain. Add the pasta to the sauce. Simmer 10 minutes. Sprinkle with grated Parmesan, if desired.

TALLERINE

Taglarini, Tell-A-Rinny, however it's spelled, this dish pops up frequently in Arkansas cookbooks, particularly from the 1950s to the 1980s. The dish of beef, noodles, black olives and such may have been named after an Italian dish brought over in the late 1890s, but by the time it began to appear under this name, it had mutated into what can be best described as a mid-century predecessor to Hamburger Helper. The entree, like many casseroles of the era, is a protein-stretcher, a kitchen sink compilation of ingredients that, except for ground beef and cheese, are all shelf-stable pantry staples.

After digging through more than 40 cookbooks with variations on the dish, I've settled on sharing this version by Martha Agee that appeared in the 1976 cookbook *Arkansas Cooking: Somehow, Somewhat, Somewhere*, published by the Washington County Unit of the American Cancer Society in Fayetteville.

1 teaspoon salt
1 pound ground beef
1 large onion, chopped
1 cup boiling water
1 clove garlic, chopped *optional*
1 cup chopped ripe olives *opt*.
1 Tablespoon Worcestershire
    sauce

1 can whole kernel corn
1-16 ounce can diced tomatoes
    undrained *or*
4 fresh tomatoes, cored and peeled
2 teaspoons chili powder
Pinch black pepper
1 package (10 ounces) pasta
1 cup shredded Cheddar

Put salt in skillet over high heat. Add ground beef, onions and garlic and brown. Add boiling water and stir in chili powder and pepper. When skillet returns to a boil, add tomatoes, corn, olives and Worcestershire sauce. Mix well.

In a separate pot, cook pasta according to directions. Drain pasta. Fold in meat mixture. Place in oblong casserole. Cover with cheese. Bake at 350°F for 30 to 45 minutes.

May be frozen; if so, bake for 1 hour and 15 minutes. Serves 4 to 6.

Variations:
1. Replace ground beef, onions and garlic with two cans chili with beans.
2. Instead of incorporating mixture with pasta, arrange over a layer of cooked spaghetti and shake on 3/4 cup Parmesan cheese.
3. Can substitute sausage for beef.

STUFFED BELL PEPPERS

Much of our fancier dinners in the 1970s consisted of things stuffed into other things - stuffed pork chops, stuffed cabbage rolls, and of course stuffed peppers, a delicacy my mom and I both enjoy to this day. It's the flavor of green pepper steak on rice, contained in a pretty little package. This version is from the Stuttgart Southland Women's Club *Talkin' About Good Cooks* cookbook, contributed by Lila Rabeneck.

1 1/2 pounds hamburger	1 1/2 cups rice, cooked
1 onion, chopped	2 cups water
7 bell peppers	6 slices cheese of choice *or*
1-16 ounce jar spaghetti sauce	1 cup grated Parmesan *optional*

Remove tops and seeds from bell peppers. Chop one bell pepper and tops of other six bell peppers. Set hollow bell peppers aside.

Saute chopped bell pepper, onion and hamburger together until beef is browned. Salt and pepper to taste. Add spaghetti sauce, water and rice. Simmer until rice is done and liquid is absorbed.

Bring water to boil in a separate pot. Boil the hollow peppers in the water for five minutes or until tender. Place in casserole dish and fill with mixture. Top with cheese if desired. Bake covered at 350°F for 30 minutes.

STUFFED BELL PEPPERS

This variation comes from *Cook's Delight: Favorite Rice Recipes Through the Years*, compiled by the Prairie County Extension Homemakers Council in 1979. This redaction is based on a recipe by Kay Moore of the Hazen Eastside Extension Homemakers Club.

4 green bell peppers	1/2 pound ground beef
1 Tablespoon butter	1 cup cooked rice
1/2 cup chopped onion	1 package cheese sauce mix
1/2 cup chopped celery	*or* 1/4 pound shredded cheese

Remove tops and seeds from bell peppers. Boil in salted water for five minutes. Set aside.

Saute onion and celery in butter. Add beef and brown. Drain well. Add rice and cheese sauce or cheese and mix thoroughly. Fill peppers. Bake at 350°F for 10-15 minutes.

PENNY SAVER BEEF SHORT RIBS

Sheila Farley's recipe appears in *A Book of Favorite Recipes* by the Cato Elementary PTA from 1976.

3 pounds beef short ribs
1 1/2 teaspoon salt
2 medium onions, sliced
1./2 teaspoon dry mustard
1 bunch/1 pound carrots
2 Tablespoons lemon juice
1/4 teaspoon pepper

1 1/2 cups water
1-10 ounce package frozen
   lima beans
2 bay leaves
1/2 cup flour
1 pound potatoes, cut into 1 1/2
   inch chunks *optional*

In a Dutch oven, brown short ribs. Save drippings. Season ribs with salt and pepper. Add onions, dry mustard, lemon juice, bay leaves, and water. Cover tightly and simmer for one hour.

Add lima beans, carrots, and potatoes (if using). Stir. Continue to simmer for another 45 minutes.

Remove and discard bay leaves. Move ribs and vegetables to heated plate.

Pour initial drippings into cooking liquid. Heat until bubbling, then whisk in flour to make gravy. Pour over ribs and vegetables before serving.

BRAISED SHORT RIBS WITH ONION GRAVY

This recipe comes from Fran Piazza, and appears in *Favorite Recipes of the Women of Good Shepherd*, printed in 1984 in Little Rock.

3 pounds beef short ribs
1/4 cup flour
1 teaspoon salt

Dash pepper
1 medium onion, sliced
1/2 cup water

Trim and reserve fat from ribs. Roll ribs in flour. Heat fat in bottom of Dutch oven. Brown ribs on all sides. Pour off fat.

Sprinkle ribs with salt and pepper. Cover with onions. Add water to Dutch oven and cover. Simmer two to two and a half hours. Add more water if needed during cooking.

Ribs are done when bone separates from meat.

Kat Robinson

POT ROAST

Common across Arkansas even today, pot roast is a time-honored tradition, a one-pot meal perfect for the end of the day. While modern cooks use Crockpots or Instapots to render tougher cuts of beef into soft, tasty bowlfuls of comfort food, cooks in earlier eras utilized Dutch ovens on the back of the stove for the same effect. This recipe from Mrs. Louise P. Gallegly appears in the 1955 book *Favorite Recipes from Clay County Kitchens*.

3 pound chuck roast	6 carrots
2 Tablespoons flour	6 medium potatoes or equivalent
Seasonings of choice	3 medium onions
2 bay leaves *optional*	1/2 teaspoon salt
3/4 cup water	1/2 teaspoon pepper

Season and dredge roast in flour. Brown well on every side in Dutch oven (if using Crockpot or Instapot, brown in skillet and transfer). Add water and bay leaves. Cover. Turn heat to high until steaming, then turn to low and cook one hour before adding vegetables.

Cut vegetables into 1 1/2 to 2 inch chunks. Season with salt and pepper. Add to top of roast - do not stir under. Recover and cook an additional 30-45 minutes or until vegetables are tender.

MEXICAN CASSEROLE

There are so many iterations and recipes listed with this name, that finding just one to exemplify over all others is difficult at best. Any dish that includes hamburger, tomatoes and cheese has the potential to qualify. This version by Syble Gwatney of Jacksonville appears in *Minute Man's Mess*, a 1977 collection of recipes from the wives of officers in the Arkansas National Guard stationed at the Jacksonville Air Force Base.

2 1/2 pounds hamburger	1 cup diced onion
6 Tablespoons chili powder	1 cup diced green bell pepper
2 teaspoons cumin	2 pounds Velveeta
1 can Ro*Tel	1 head lettuce, chopped
1 or 2 tomatoes, diced	1 large bag Doritos

Brown meat. Add onions and pepper, season and let simmer. Cut cheese into cubes and melt with Ro*Tel. Layer lettuce and tomato in large dish. Add crumbled Doritos, then meat mixture. Cover with melted cheese dip and serve immediately. Feeds 8 to 12.

CORNED BEEF AND CABBAGE

A dish best represented in Arkansas cookbooks of the 1950s-1970s, this dish is made easier today thanks to pre-packaged ready-to-prepare vacuum sealed bags in the meat aisle. But corning, or salting, a brisket was once a popular dish here. This redaction comes from a 1971 recipe by Mrs. Rayburn J. Edgar from *The King's Collection: Favorite Recipes from Christ The King Church.*

4-5 pounds beef brisket	2 bell peppers, sliced into rings
1/2 onion	1/2 teaspoon rosemary *optional*
4 cloves	1 stalk celery
6 peppercorns	1 carrot
1 bay leaf	3 sprigs fresh parsley
2 cloves garlic, quartered	1 cabbage, cored and quartered

Place brisket in Dutch oven and cover with cold water. Add all other ingredients except cabbage. Bring to a boil for five minutes. Remove scum that rises to the top. Cover and simmer 3-5 hours or until tender.

Uncover and top with cabbage wedges. Cover and cook 20 minutes more. Allow meat to rest 20 minutes, then slice and serve with cabbage and mustard sauce.

2 Tablespoons butter or olive oil	1 teaspoon salt
Dash black pepper	1 egg yolk
1 Tablespoon prepared mustard	3/4 cup milk
1 Tablespoon flour	2 teaspoons lemon juice

Melt butter in double boiler. Stir in next four ingredients. Beat egg yolk into milk and add into mixture. Continue to stir over heat until sauce thickens, about five minutes. Remove from heat. Add lemon juice just before serving.

TUNA CASSEROLE

Mary Ann Sellick of the Berryville Future Business Leaders of America chapter contributed the original recipe to the *Arkansas FB-LA-PBL Cookbook*.

1 can tuna	2 chicken bouillon cubes
1 can cream of chicken soup	1/2 cup grated cheese
1 small bag noodles	1 can English peas *optional*

Boil noodles in salted water; drain. Combine soup and one soup can water. Dissolve bouillon in soup mixture. Combine noodles, soup mixture, tuna, and peas if using. Place in greased casserole. Bake at 350°F for 25 minutes. Sprinkle cheese on top and bake until cheese melts.

CHICKEN SPAGHETTI

A dish that has evolved over the decades, this combination of starch and protein remains a popular lunchroom dish across the state. While today's versions are often an amalgamation of spaghetti noodles, pulled chicken and Velveeta cheese dip, the dish originated as a far more complex yet just as filling construction. This redaction comes from a version by Mrs. Worth James appeared in the 1954 cookbook from the Women's Society of Christian Service chapter at Asbury Methodist Church in Little Rock.

1 large hen	5 cloves garlic, minced
Salt and pepper	1-15 ounce can tomatoes
2-12 ounce packages spaghetti	1-7 ounce can tomato paste
2 Tablespoons butter	3 sprigs parsley, minced
1 green bell pepper, diced	4 Tablespoons chili powder
4 stalks celery, diced	1-4 ounce can sliced mushrooms
3 large onions, diced	3 bay leaves

Season hen with salt and pepper. Boil hen until meat falls off the bone. Remove chicken from pot and reserve broth. De-bone and chop meat. Refrigerate meat until ready to add. Return broth to a boil and add spaghetti. Boil until spaghetti is tender. Drain.

While spaghetti is cooking, heat butter in skillet. Add bell pepper, celery and onions and cook until onions are translucent. Add garlic, tomatoes in their juice, tomato paste, parsley and chili powder. Let simmer 15 minutes. Remove from heat and stir in mushrooms and bay leaves. Let rest while boiling spaghetti.

After draining spaghetti, fold in chicken. Remove bay leaves from sauce and add sauce to spaghetti, stirring well. Garnish with Parmesan cheese if desired and serve immediately.

OR - turn spaghetti out into baking dish. Top with 1 cup mozzarella and 1/2 cup Parmesan. Bake at 350°F for 25 minutes. Serve hot.

KING RANCH CHICKEN CASSEROLE

Variations on this recipe appear in dozens of early 1980s cookbooks, including three different iterations in the 1984 *St. James Family Cookbook*, put together by the Christian Mothers Fellowship at St. James United Methodist Church in Little Rock. This is Connie Bullock's version.

1 chicken	1 can cream of chicken soup
3 Tablespoons oil	1 teaspoon oregano
1 onion, diced	1 teaspoon cumin
1 green bell pepper, diced	1 teaspoon chili powder
1 can Ro*Tel	1 Tablespoon butter
1 cup chicken broth	1 package tortillas
1 can cream of mushroom soup	1 cup shredded Cheddar

Boil, de-bone and dice chicken, reserving one cup broth. Saute pepper and onion in oil. Bring all remaining ingredients except tortillas to a boil in a saucepan, stirring frequently. Remove from heat. Grease a casserole with butter. Alternate layers of tortillas and chicken. Pour sauce over top and sprinkle cheese over all. Bake 45 minutes at 350°F. Let stand 20 minutes before serving.

CHICKEN IN MUSTARD SAUCE

Mrs. L. W. Walters submitted this recipe to the 1967 *Fine Foods* cookbook by the Osceola Progressives Club.

4 whole chicken breasts, de-boned and skinned	1/2 teaspoon garlic salt
	1/2 teaspoon onion salt
1/2 cup flour	4 Tablespoons butter
1 teaspoon seasoned salt	

Split breasts to form eight servings, reserve bones and skin. Mix flour and salts; dip each breast portion in flour mix. Brown each side in hot butter in pan, about five minutes to each side. Keep hot.

Boil bones and skin to make 1 1/2 cups broth - OR, use two chicken bouillon cubes in 1 1/2 cups boiling water.

1 Tablespoon lemon juice	1 Tablespoons corn starch
1 1/2 teaspoon dry mustard	2 Tablespoons water
2 teaspoons sugar	

Mix ingredients together and add to boiling broth. Cook through until thickened. Pour gravy over chicken. Garnish with parsley.

CHINESE CHICKEN

Listed as O-No O-No, this dish was contributed by Joyce Mayo in the 1979 collection *Foods of Note* by the Fort Smith Symphony Guild.

1/4 cup margarine or butter	1 can sliced water chestnuts
4 green onions, chopped	1-4 ounce can sliced mushrooms
1 clove garlic, pressed	1 can bamboo shoots
2 Tablespoons flour	1-20 ounce can pineapple chunks
1 teaspoon soy sauce	3 cups cooked chicken, diced
1 cup sauterne or white wine	1 small jar pimentos

In stainless steel skillet, combine butter, green onions, garlic, flour, soy sauce and white wine, stirring frequently until sauce is thickened.

Add remaining ingredients and cook together until sauce clings to chicken. Serve over rice or noodles. Top with macadamia nuts..

GLORIFIED CHICKEN

Mrs. J.E. Willman's recipe stretches the definition of chicken.

1 pound veal	1 egg, well beaten
1 pound pork	Salt

Cheap cuts, cook until done and then grind - save broth. Make into loaf and put broth in with mixture. Bake in pan of water until it leaves sides of dish.

FRIED CHICKEN

This recipe by Jeannette Burns appears in *Recipes You Can Bank On*, shared in the 1970s by the Bank of West Memphis. I present it in the original text.

Girls! Go to the store and BUY A CHICKEN. Don't attempt to kill, pick and clean it yourselves. It's bad enough to have to wash and skin the thing without having to kill it, too.

Wash and pull the skin off the chicken. Some of you may like the skin, but did you know it is very fattening? Take a cup of flour, salt and pepper to taste and mix it together. I use a large Ziplock bag to put my flour in and shake the chicken in this until it is well coated with flour.

In a skillet, melt a cup and a half of Crisco (or oil). Put chicken into the hot oil and cook at a medium heat with a top on the skillet until chicken is tender and brown. Girls, you will have to turn the chicken over in order for it to turn brown on both sides. Remove from skillet and put chicken on a dish with a paper towel to absorb the grease. Very good.

P.S. I have made all of these recipes as simple as I could with the thought of a young lady just beginning to cook or a newlywed with no knowledge of soup from steak or venison from chicken. Happy eating.

Kat Robinson

80

WAVA'S SOUR CREAM ENCHILADAS

Another from *Cornerstone Cookery*, put out by the St. Vincent's Infirmary Employee Council. We used to make this in big batches to freeze, because estimating the amount of sauce needed was tough. You can substitute shredded cooked chicken for the ground beef, or omit it and use roasted sweet peppers and mushrooms.

1 1.2 pounds ground beef	1-16 ounce tub sour cream
2 onions, diced	30 corn or flour tortillas,
2 cans cream of chicken soup	10 inches in diameter
2 cans cream of mushroom soup	2 pounds sharp Cheddar, grated

Brown ground beef and onion together and drain. In medium saucepan, combine soups and sour cream. Do not boil. Warm tortillas in oven for 8-10 minutes.

For each enchilada: Place one tablespoon each of meat mix and soup mix and spread 2 teaspoons of cheese from end to end. Fold sides in and roll. Place seam side down in greased casserole dishes (it will fill two 9x13 pans). Pour remaining soup mix over top, then sprinkle with cheese. Bake at 250°F. 30-40 minutes or until edges of tortillas begin to brown.

Unbaked pans of enchiladas can be frozen and baked later. To cook, defrost in refrigerator overnight, then follow baking directions.

CREAMED CHICKEN WITH BISCUITS

Rema O'Brien of Southside Baptist Church contributed this recipe to *Feeding Your Neighbor* by Pine Bluff's Neighbor to Neighbor project.

2 cups cooked, diced chicken	1/3 cup chopped pimento
1 quart chicken broth	1 small onion, grated
1/2 cup butter	salt and pepper to taste
1/2 cup flour	One recipe biscuits, unbaked
1 can cream of mushroom soup	(canned or recipe from page 51)

Melt butter, stir in flour until smooth. Add broth and soup, stirring until well blended. Add remaining ingredients. Pour into lightly greased 9x13 baking dish and top with uncooked biscuits. Bake at 450°F. for 10-12 minutes or until biscuits have cooked. Serves 8.

SQUASH AND SAUSAGE CASSEROLE

The American Cancer Society Arkansas Division put out an excellent cookbook in 1983 called *Sampling Arkansas*. This recipe from George Vaught of the Perry Unit is really, really good - a meal in itself.

4 cups cooked, drained and chopped squash	2 eggs, beaten
	1/2 cup sugar
1 medium onion, diced	1 teaspoon salt
12 crackers, crumbled	1/2 pound cooked sausage,
1/2 cup shredded Cheddar cheese	crumbled
	1/4 cup melted butter

In a large mixing bowl, combine all ingredients in order listed, reserving half the cheese. Pour into well-greased two quart baking dish and sprinkle with reserved cheese. Bake at 350°F for 30 minutes or until lightly browned and bubbly. Serves 4-6.

BAKED PORK CHOPS

These two recipes come from the book *Kitchen Kapers*, published in 1952 by the Riceland Garden Club Members of Stuttgart.

6 pork chops cut 1 inch thick	flour
6 slices pineapple	salt, pepper and celery salt to taste

Blend together flour and spices. Dredge each pork chop with the dry mix, then arrange in shallow pan. Bake in hot oven (400°F) and baste with 1 teaspoon of water on each chop. After 30 minutes, add one slice of pineapple to each chop and bake 15 minutes longer.

HILO HAWAIIAN SPARE RIBS

This recipe from Kitchen Kapers includes a popular 50s blend of ketchup, Worcestershire sauce and red pepper flakes to invoke a Polynesian flavor.

2 medium onions, sliced	1/2 teaspoon black pepper
1 teaspoon chili powder	5 pounds spare ribs
1/2 teaspoon red pepper flakes	2 Tablespoons vinegar
2 Tablespoons Worcestershire sauce	1 Tablespoon salt
	3/4 cup water
3/4 cup ketchup	1 teaspoon paprika

Cut ribs into two rib sections. Sprinkle with salt, pepper and flour. Place in roaster and cover with sliced onions. Mix remaining ingredients together and pour over ribs in roaster. Cover and bake in 350°F oven for three hours. Baste occasionally, turning meat once or twice. Remove cover during last 15 minutes.

HAM AND POTATO CASSEROLE

This filling dish that can be breakfast or dinner in itself was contributed by Melba Clark to *Delights of the Delta II* by the Chicot County 4-H and Extension Homemakers Clubs.

3 cups thinly sliced potatoes	1/8 teaspoon black pepper
1 cup diced ham	1 1/2 teaspoons salt
1 cup grated cheese	2 Tablespoons oleo or butter
1/2 large onion, minced	1/2 cup flour
2 cups milk	

Melt butter in saucepan. Add onion and cook until tender. Stir in salt, pepper, and flour. Slowly add milk. Cook until thickens. Remove from heat and stir in cheese. In a buttered casserole dish, put half of raw potatoes, half of cheese sauce, all of ham, then rest of potatoes and rest of cheese sauce. Bake covered one to one and a half hours at 350°F.

HASHBROWN CASSEROLE

This recipe was on a torn slip of paper tucked in the back of a Farm Bureau cookbook.

1/2 Tablespoon butter	1/2 teaspoon minced garlic
1 onion, diced	1 package frozen hashbrowns,
1 can cream of celery soup	thawed
8 ounces Monterrey Jack	salt and pepper to taste
16 ounces sour cream	1 cup crushed potato chips

Saute onion in butter. Mix in soup, cheese, sour cream, and garlic. Fold in hashbrowns. Season with salt and pepper to taste. Place in greased 9x13 casserole dish and cover with crushed potato chips. Bake 35-40 minutes at 350°F or until potatoes are tender and top browns.

BARBECUE

Anne Bailey shared this recipe in *Recipes You Can Bank On* from the Bank of West Memphis.

3 pounds ground beef	1 1/2 cups brown sugar
1 onion, chopped fine	3 1/2 tablespoons table mustard
1 Tablespoon vinegar	1-12 ounce bottle ketchup
1 1/2 Tablespoons	salt and pepper to taste
Worcestershire sauce	

Brown meat and onion. Combine all other ingredients. Pour off drippings from meat. Add sauce mixture to meat and simmer 1 1/2 hours. Tastes better if it sits another hour before serving.

85

SIDE DISHES

OKRA STIR FRY

Rowlena Bell of the Greenbrier Extension Homemakers Club contributed this recipe to the Faulkner County Extension Home-makers Council's 1987 cookbook *Thank Heavens for Homemade Cooks.*

2 cups okra, sliced 1/2 inch thick
1 small onion, sliced
1 green bell pepper, diced
1/2 cup diced celery
1/2 teaspoon salt

1/8 teaspoon black pepper
1/4 teaspoon thyme
3 Tablespoons vegetable oil
1 medium tomato cut into wedges
soy sauce to taste

Stir fry okra, onion, bell pepper, celery, salt, pepper and thyme in hot oil over high heat. Stir six to 10 minutes. Add tomatoes and stir fry two more minutes. Sprinkle with soy sauce to taste.

BAKED TOMATOES

The 1976 cookbook Recipes from Arkansas by the School Food Service Association is an excellent repository of mid-century recipes like this one by Margaret Caldwell of Oak Grove Elementary.

6 tomatoes
1/4 cup chopped green peppers
3/4 cups cooked corn
1 teaspoon salt

1/4 teaspoon black pepper
6 Tablespoons bread crumbs
6 teaspoons butter

Cut tops from tomatoes and remove pulp, leaving a shell 1/4 inch thick. Cover green peppers with boiling water and let sit five minutes. Drain. Mix tomato pulp, green pepper, corn and seasonings. Fiill tomato shells and cover each with bread crumbs. Dot each one with butter. Bake at 375°F for 20 minutes.

89

TOMATO ZUCCHINI CHEESE CASSEROLE

Myrtle Jordan's recipe in *Kissin' Wears Out, Cookin' Don't* by the Levy Baptist Church Baptist Young Women is an utter summer delight.

2 pounds fresh tomatoes, sliced
1 pound zucchini, thinly sliced
2 cups shredded Muenster cheese

1 teaspoon salt
1/4 teaspoon black pepper
2 Tablespoons butter

Preheat oven to 350°F. In two quart casserole, layer tomatoes, zucchini, and cheese. Sprinkle each layer with a little salt and pepper. Finish with cheese. Dot top with butter. Cover with foil. Bake 45 minutes. Remove foil. Bake another 10 minutes or until vegetables are tender. Serves 4-6.

EGGPLANT CASSEROLE

There are dozens upon dozens of versions of this dish, usually attributed to the much-missed Franke's Cafeteria, once Arkansas's oldest continuously operating cafeteria. This version is by Minnie Beth White and appears in *Primrose Cooks* by the Primrose United Methodist Church of Little Rock.

1 medium eggplant	1 cup grated Parmesan
1 medium onion	2 eggs
2 Tablespoons butter	1 cup bread crumbs
1/2 cup tomatoes	

Pare eggplant into 1 inch cubes. Cook in a little water. Drain and cool. Season with salt and pepper. Cook tomatoes and onion in butter together. Add cheese, eggs and half the bread crumbs. Lay eggplant into greased casserole. Top with tomato mixture, then rest of bread crumbs. Bake at 350°F until top begins to brown.

FRIED CABBAGE

Bertha Ayers contributed this recipe to the 1972 book *Favorite Hometown Recipes*.

1 head cabbage	1 diced green hot pepper
1/4 cup water	1 teaspoon sugar
1 stick oleo or butter	salt and pepper to taste

Dice a head of cabbage coarsely. Put in frying pan and add water. Add rest of ingredients, cover and simmer until tender. Remove cover and cook until almost dry.

WHITE RIVER FRIED POTATOES

A standard breakfast side that works well with fish dinners, too, this skillet-fried potato dish was contributed by John Woodard to the Pike View Elementary 1980 cookbook.

5 large new potatoes	1/2 teaspoon salt
or equivalent	1 teaspoon paprika
peanut oil for skillet	1/8 teaspoon red pepper flakes
1/2 teaspoon black pepper	1 large white onion

Peel potatoes if you wish. Wash and dry potatoes and onion. Cut into 1/2 inch chunks. Put into cold skillet with oil. Add salt and pepper. Fry moderately until potatoes begin to brown. Add paprika and red pepper flakes. Continue to cook, stirring frequently. Add 1/2 cup water, turn and cover.

Cook over low heat 10 minutes, then remove cover. Increase heat and brown. Remove from heat and serve.

POTATO PATTIES

A fun dish by the Kommon Cents Kookin' Club's 1978 cookbook.

2 cups prepared mashed potatoes   Salt and pepper to taste
1/4 cup flour   Hot oil for frying

Mix potatoes, flour, salt and pepper together. Drop by spoonfuls into hot oil, pressing flat with back of spatula. Turn once.

FRIED ZUCCHINI

A great way to get your child to eat zucchini, this batter can also be used to fry eggplant, yellow squash or okra.

3-4 zucchini, cut into planks   1 egg
1 sleeve saltine crackers   1 cup milk
1/2 cup flour   1 teaspoon hot sauce
1/2 teaspoon salt   Oil for frying
1/2 teaspoon black pepper

Pound saltine crackers into crumbs and mix with flour, salt and pepper. Place in ziptop bag. Beat egg with milk and hot sauce. in bowl large enough to submerge zucchini planks.

Bring oil to medium heat. One at a time, dip zucchini in egg wash and drop into ziptop bag. Shake bag. With tongs, remove each zucchini plank and place in hot oil. Fry til brown, then flip. Remove to paper towel lined plate. Serve hot.

SQUASH CASSEROLE

A delightful alternative to dressing to go along with chicken or turkey. The original recipe comes from *SCAT Cook's*, by Senior Citizens Activity Today, Inc. in Little Rock.

6 to 8 yellow squash, sliced   1 cup chopped celery
1 medium onion, diced   3/4 cup sour cream
1/2 stick butter or oleo   salt and pepper to taste
1 teaspoon sugar

Cook squash, celery and onion in butter. Combine sour cream, sugar, salt and pepper and fold into squash. Place in oven-safe small casserole and bake at 350°F for 15 to 20 minutes.

GREEN RICE

Found in more than 100 different cookbooks of the era, this delicacy utilizes an Arkansas staple as the perfect savory side starch. This iteration comes, appropriately enough, from the Chicot County 4-H and Extension Homemakers Club's *Delights From the Delta II* cookbook.

4 cups cooked rice   2-4 ounce cans mushrooms
3 eggs   1 large onion, minced
2/3 cups vegetable oil   2 cups chopped broccoli
1 can PET milk   2 stalks celery, minced
3 cups sharp Cheddar   salt and pepper to taste
2 cans cream of mushroom soup

Beat eggs and add oil. Add this and all other ingredients to cooked rice. Bake in greased, shallow casserole at 350°F for 45 minutes. Serves 10. Can be frozen.

HAM AND POTATO SALAD

Faye Crews assembled the tiny but fine collection Arkansas Country Cooking in 1981 - where you can find this splendid offering. It works as a light lunch on its own or a substantial side dish.

1/2 cup sour cream

2 Tablespoons vinegar

1/2 teaspoon salt

2 Tablespoons milk

2 green onions, thinly sliced

1 boiled egg, diced

1 1/2 cups diced ham

2 cups cooked potato, diced

1/2 teaspoon black pepper

1 carrot, coarsely shredded

1/2 cup cottage cheese

1/2 cup diced celery

Mix together sour cream, salt, pepper, vinegar and milk. Combine remaining ingredients. Fold both mixes together. Chill for one hour.

LIMA BEANS WITH DILL

This recipe appears in the 1984 book *Favorite Recipes of the Women of Good Shepherd*, published by The Episcopal Church of the Good Shepherd in Little Rock.

2 pounds lima beans
4 Tablespoons olive oil
1 Tablespoon lime juice

2 Tablespoons chopped fresh
   dill *or* 2 Tablespoons dill
   seeds, crushed

Steam lima beans for 20 minutes or until tender. Heat remaining ingredients and pour over lima beans. Serves 6.

LIMA BEANS WITH HAM

This hot dish is found in several cookbooks across the state throughout the 20th Century.

1 1/2 pounds lima beans
1/2 pound ham
1 Tablespoon black pepper

2 Tablespoons butter
1 teaspoon red pepper flakes
1 teaspoon dry parsley

Soak lima beans for 30 minutes or until tender. Drain. In a deep skillet, fry ham. Add remaining ingredients and stir until butter melts. Pour lima beans into skillet and saute until lima beans mash with a press by the back of a spoon. Serve hot.

SAVORY BROCCOLI

This recipe, attributed to Mrs. Pearrow, appears in the 1976 cookbook *From Temple's Cupboard*, compiled by the Newlywed Sunday School Class at Temple Baptist Church in southwest Little Rock.

1-10 ounce package frozen broccoli	1 clove garlic, minced
4 slices bacon	2 Tablespoons butter
1 small onion, chopped	2 Tablespoons flour
	1 cup milk

Cook broccoli according to instructions on package. Fry bacon until crisp. Remove, drain and crumble. Add onion and garlic to skillet until onion yellows. Add butter and melt. Stir in flour and make a roux. Gradually stir in milk and keep stirring until thickened. Add broccoli and bacon and season to taste.

PECAN SWEET POTATOES

This is my mom's recipe, found in *Cornerstone Cookery*, which she edited for the St. Vincent Infirmary Employee Council in 1984.

2 eggs	3 cups sweet potatoes, cooked and mashed
1 cup sugar	
3/4 cup butter or margarine	1 cup brown sugar
1/2 cup milk	2 Tablespoons butter or margarine
1 teaspoon vanilla	1/3 cup flour
	1 cup chopped pecans

Blend all ingredients in left column. Stir into sweet potatoes and place in a greased casserole. Mix brown sugar, butter and flour and spread over sweet potatoes, then top with nuts. Bake at 350°F for one hour.

SQUAW CORN

Similar to calico corn, this version of the dish was submitted by Judy Murphree to *Favorite Hometown Recipes*, compiled by the Senior Womens Ministries Class of Glad Tidings Assembly of God Church in North Little Rock.

6 slices bacon
4 eggs, well beaten
1 small onion, diced
1 green bell pepper, diced

1 red bell pepper, diced
1-15 ounce can whole kernel corn
3 Tablespoons butter
salt and pepper to taste

Fry bacon until crisp; remove bacon from pan. Fry onions and peppers in grease. Drain and return to pan. Add corn and juice in can. When corn comes to a boil, gradually add eggs, stirring gently and constantly. Crumble bacon. Add bacon, butter, salt and pepper and cook until consistency of scrambled eggs.

CARROT CASSEROLE

Eleanor Shumate of the Andante Music Club offered this recipe to the Arkansas Federation of Music Club's 1984 *Musicians and the Culinary Arts* cookbook.

3 cups sliced carrots
6 soda crackers, crushed
1 teaspoon onion or garlic salt

1/4 cup chopped green pepper
2 Tablespoons melted butter
1/2 cup grated sharp Cheddar

Cook carrots 10 minutes over medium heat. Combine cracker crumbs, onion or garlic salt and green bell pepper. Alternate layers of carrots and crumbs in 8x8 baking dish. Add butter to cooking liquid and heat until butter is melted. Pour over carrots and top with cheese. Bake at 425°F for 15 to 20 minutes.

GREAT NORTHERN BEAN CASSEROLE

This recipe by Mrs. Bernice Emeragn was on an index card in a box on a shelf behind the kitchen door at my maternal grandmother's house.

1 1/2 cups dried northern beans
1/2 pound sliced bacon
2 medium onions, diced

1 green bell pepper, sliced
1 cup hot diluted PET milk
(half PET milk, half water)

Soak beans overnight. Cook until tender. Drain. Cut bacon into small pieces and saute in a hot frying pan. Remove bacon; add pepper and onion and cook until tender. In a buttered casserole, layer beans, bacon and onions and peppers. Pour over PET milk mix. Bake at 400°F for 20-30 minutes. Serve hot.

DESSERTS

Kat Robinson

104

RAW APPLE CAKE

I found this recipe from Susie Rochier in the 1979 cookbook by the Circle of Hope from the First Church of the Nazarene in Fayetteville. It's so craveable, I had to give away most of this cake so I wouldn't eat it in a sitting. You can make it with most any sort of apple. I used a variety of Honeycrisp, Fuji and Granny Smith to get a lovely balance of tart and sweet within the flavor, but feel free to select apples to your own tastes.

1 cup vegetable or canola oil	2 cups all-purpose flour
1 cup sugar	1 teaspoon soda
1 cup brown sugar	1/2 teaspoon salt
2 eggs	1 cup chopped pecans
2 teaspoons vanilla extract	1 cup raisins
	4 cups diced apple

Cream together oil, sugars, eggs and vanilla extract. Sift together flour, salt and soda. Add to creamed mixture. Fold in nuts, raisins and apples. Bake in greased 9 x 11 pan at 325 degrees for 40 minutes, or a Bundt cake pan for 55-60 minutes.

Note: An inserted toothpick will come out wet when inserted, even if the cake is done. Look for a clear, wet toothpick; a cloudy wet toothpick indicates the batter is not completely cooked through.

Excellent served with coffee, even better with fresh whipped cream.

COCA-COLA CAKE

A personal favorite of mine, this rich but light cake is a lovely informal choice for your sideboard. While the tradition is to ice the cake in the pan, I have discovered the joys of the combination of hot icing and cold milk. That subtle Coke flavor is enticing, particularly amongst those who have never encountered this delicacy.

Cake:

2 cups unsifted flour
2 cups sugar
2 sticks oleo or butter
3 Tablespoons cocoa
1 cup Coca-Cola
2 eggs

1/2 cup buttermilk
  OR 1/2 cup milk plus 1.5
  teaspoons lemon juice
1 teaspoon baking soda
1 teaspoon vanilla
1 1/2 cups mini marshmallows

Heat oven to 350°F. If planning to ice cake, spread pecans from recipe below on sheet pan and slide into oven, removing when oven has reached desired temperature.

Combine flour and sugar. Heat butter, cocoa and Coke to boiling and pour over flour and sugar mixture. Beat eggs; add buttermilk or substitute, lemon juice, baking soda and vanilla and mix well. Add marshmallows. Combine with other ingredients.

Grease a large flat pan. Turn out batter and even out to one inch in depth. Bake at 350°F for 30-35 or until a toothpick inserted in the middle comes out clean. Have icing prepared for pour-over, if using.

Icing:

1/2 cup oleo or butter
3 Tablespoons cocoa
6 Tablespoons Coca-Cola

1 box (16 ounces) confectioner's
  sugar
1 cup chopped pecans

Combine butter, cocoa and Coca-Cola and bring to a boil. Pour over confectioner's sugar. Beat well. Stir in toasted pecans.

Option 1 (traditional): While cake is still in pan, pour icing over and smooth. When cake is cool, slice as desired.

Option 2 (21st century): Allow cake to cool after baking. Slice cake as desired. Assemble and heat icing and pour over individual slices. Serve immediately.

FRUIT COCKTAIL CAKE

This very moist, rich cake begins with a mix - but becomes something much more. Substitute a pound cake recipe if you wish for extra richness. The original comes from Marlene Reddig and appears in *Our Best To You*, the 1984 cookbook by the Park Hill Baptist Church in North Little Rock.

1 box yellow cake mix	1 1/2 cups sugar
1/2 cup vegetable oil	3/4 cup evaporated milk
3 eggs	nuts and coconut if desired
1 can fruit cocktail	
1 stick butter	

Mix cake mix, oil, eggs and fruit cocktail. Turn into greased Bundt cake pan and bake 35-45 minutes at 350°F.

While cake is baking, bring butter, sugar and milk in a saucepan to a boil. When the cake comes out of the oven, prick the top all over with a toothpick, then drizzle the butter melt all over. Adorn with nuts and coconut if you wish.

FRUIT COBBLER

I found this recipe on a scrap of paper in one of the many cookbooks in my collection.	1 cup flour 1 cup sugar 1 cup milk	1/2 stick butter 1 can or 1 pack-aage frozen fruit

Mix flour, sugar and milk together until smooth. Melt butter in pan and pour in mixture. Top with canned peaches (or any can or 10 ounce package of fruit). Bake at 350°F for 40 minutes.

1 cup Flour
1 cup sugar
1 cup milk
1/4 cup Butter
1 large can peaches

mix Flour, sugar, milk until smooth
Melt Butter in pan and peach to mixture pour in pan

WATERGATE CAKE

Mildred Anderson of Immanuel Baptist Church shared this cover-up cake recipe with the Neighbor to Neighbor Program in Pine Bluff for the cookbook *Feeding Your Neighbor*.

1 box white cake mix	10 ounces 7-Up
3 eggs	or lemon-lime soda
3/4 cup vegetable oil	1/2 cup coconut
1 package pistachio pudding	

Beat eggs well. Add oil and 7-Up; mix well. Add cake mix, then other ingredients. Pour into greased 9x13 pan and bake at 350°F for 45-60 minutes. Cool before frosting.

2 envelopes Dream Whip	1/2 cup coconut
1 package pistachio pudding	3/4 cup chopped pecans
1 1/2 cups cold milk	

Beat Dream Whip, pudding and milk with mixer until thick. Fold in half of the coconut and pecans. Spread on cooled cake. Sprinkle the rest of the coconut and nuts on top. Refrigerate until ready to serve.

LEMON CHESS PIE

Miss Eloise Rhode contributed this recipe, which her mom wrote down in 1971, to *A Dash of This, A Pinch of That*. It's a lovely, rich pie.

Crust	Filling
1 cup flour	2 cups sugar
1/2 cup shortening	1 stick oleo or butter
1/2 teaspoon salt	4 eggs (add one at a time)
few Tablespoons ice water	1/2 cup lemon juice
	1 rounded Tablespoon flour

Mix flour, shortening and salt thoroughly. Add just enough ice water to be able to roll out a 9" crust. Lay crust across pan and refrigerate.

Beat all filling ingredients together until smooth. Pour into unbaked pie crust. Bake at 400°F a few minutes, then turn down to 350°F and bake until firm.

NO CRUST COCONUT PIE

In 1975, Mrs. James S. Grisham contributed this recipe to the Cato Elementary PTA's cookbook *Favorite Dishes From Our Best Cooks*.

1/4 cup butter or margarine	1/4 cup self-raising flour
1 cup sugar	1/2 can (3 1/2 ounce) flaked
2 eggs	coconut
1 cup milk	nutmeg

Cream butter and sugar. Add eggs one at a time, mixing well after each egg. Add milk and flour, blend well. Add coconut. Pour into lightly greased and floured 9" pie pan. Sprinkle with nutmeg. Bake at 350°F for 45 minutes or until set.

STRAWBERRY BLUEBERRY PIE

This recipe was redacted from one for strawberry pie by Neal Hart in the 1970 book *Cook's Delight* by the Victory Baptist Elementary Parent Teacher Fellowship. I augmented by replacing half the strawberries called for with blueberries - fresh is OK, frozen works great.

1 pound frozen strawberries
1 pound frozen blueberries
1/2 teaspoon lemon juice
2 Tablespoons cornstarch
1.4 teaspoon salt

1 cup juice drained from
   defrosted fruit (add water to
   equal 1 cup if necessary)
1/4 cup sugar
baked pie shell
whipped cream for garnish

Defrost fruit in package. Drain juice from fruit. Sprinkle lemon juice over fruit. Blend cornstarch, salt and sugar in saucepan. Stir in fruit juice. Cook, stirring constantly, until thickened. Let cool. Arrange fruit in pie crust. Pour cooled sauce over fruit. Chill at least three hours in refrigerator. Garnish with whipped cream.

RECIPES A–Z

KING RANCH CHICKEN
   CASSEROLE 77
LAYERED TACO DIP 26
LEMON CHESS PIE 111
LIMA BEANS WITH DILL
   99
LIMA BEANS WITH HAM
   99
MARINATED SALAD 22
MEXICAN CASSEROLE 73
MOLASSES BREAD 40
NO CRUST COCONUT PIE
   112
OKRA STIR FRY 88
OLD FASHION BREAD
   PUDDING 59
ONION-RICE OMELET 48
ORANGE MUFFINS 56
ORANGE SALAD 17
OZARK BREAD PUDDING
   59
PARTY BISCUITS 51
PECAN SWEET POTATOES
   100
PENNY SAVER BEEF
   SHORT RIBS 70
POTATO PATTIES 94
POT ROAST 73
PUMPKIN BREAD 37
QUICHE LORRAINE 56
QUICK APPLE-CELERY
   SALAD 14
RAW APPLE CAKE 105
FRUIT SALAD 13
SALMON CROQUETTES 31
SALSA 26
SAUSAGE CREAM GRAVY
   ON BISCUITS 53

SAVORY BROCCOLI 100
SHRIMP DIP 28
SIX WEEK BRAN MUFFINS
   54
SPINACH QUICHE 56
SQUASH AND SAUSAGE
   CASSEROLE 83
SQUASH CASSEROLE 96
SQUASH FRITTERS 25
SQUAW CORN 101
STRAWBERRY BLUEBERRY
   PIE 113
STRAWBERRY SALAD 17
STUFFED BELL PEPPERS
   69
STUFFED CUCUMBERS 21
TALLERINE 67
THREE BEAN SALAD 24
TOMATO FRITATTA 48
TOMATO SOUP SALAD 19
TOMATO ZUCCHINI
   CHEESE CASSEROLE
   90
TUNA CASSEROLE 75
UNCOOKED STRAWBERRY
   PRESERVES 52
WALDORF SALAD 14
WATERGATE CAKE 110
WAVA'S SOUR CREAM
   ENCHILADAS 81
WHITE RIVER FRIED
   POTATOES 93
YEAST BISCUITS 51
ZUCCHINI BREAD 40
ZUCCHINI SALAD 15

Kat Robinson is Arkansas's food historian and most enthusiastic road warrior. The Little Rock-based author is the host of the Emmy-nominated documentary *Make Room For Pie; A Delicious Slice of The Natural State* and the Arkansas PBS show *Home Cooking with Kat and Friends*, as well as the filmmaker of the 2021 documentary *Arkansas Dairy Bars: Neat Eats and Cool Treats*. She is a member of the Arkansas Food Hall of Fame committee, a co-chair of the Arkansas Pie Festival, and the Arkansas fellow to the National Food and Beverage Museum.

She has written eleven books on food, most notably *Arkansas Food: The A to Z of Eating in The Natural State*, an alphabetic guide to the dishes, delights and food traditions that define her home state. Two of her more recent travel guides, *101 Things to Eat in Arkansas Before You Die* and *102 More Things to Eat in Arkansas Before You Die* define the state's most iconic and trusted eateries. Robinson's *Another Slice of Arkansas Pie: A Guide to the Best Restaurants, Bakeries, Truck Stops and Food Trucks for Delectable Bites in The Natural State* outlines more than 400 places to find the dessert, an extraordinary accomplishment that took thousands of miles, hundreds of hours and so many bites to properly document and catalogue.

In this book, *Arkansas Cookery: Retro Recipes from The Natural State*. Robinson examines mid-century cookbooks from all over Arkansas. Her collection of more than 400 20th Century cookbooks and research into shared recipes, cooking methods and flavors of the era has been brought together for this lovingly photographed collection of foods previous generations brought to the table. The recipes are all redacted and were prepared on location at The Writer's Colony at Dairy Hollow in Eureka Springs, The nostalgic *Arkansas Dairy Bars: Neat Eats and Cool Treats*, the companion book for the film of the same name, is her other 2021 work.

Robinson shares her personal life experiences in *A Bite of Arkansas: A Cookbook of Natural State Delights*, her 2020 culinary memoir, which offers 140 recipes made by and photographed herself. She also edited and contributed to the collection *43 Tables: An Internet Community Cooks During Quarantine*.

Kat Robinson's work has appeared in regional and national publications including *Food Network, Forbes Travel Guide, Serious Eats*, and *AAA Magazines*, among others. Her expertise in food research and Arkansas restaurants has been cited by *Saveur, Eater, USA Today, The Wall Street Journal, The Outline*, and the Southern Foodways Alliance's *Gravy* podcast, for her skills and talents related to food research and documentation.

Her efforts have been celebrated in articles by *Arkansas Good Roads, Arkansas Business, 501 Life Magazine*, the *Northwest Arkansas Democrat-Gazette* and the *Arkansas Democrat-Gazette*. She has served as the keynote speaker for the South Arkansas Literary Festival and the Arkansas Library Association Conference and has spoken at the Six Bridges Literary Festival, Eureka Springs Books in Bloom and the Fayetteville True Lit Festival.

While she writes on food and travel subjects throughout the United States, she is best known for her ever-expanding knowledge of Arkansas food history and restaurant culture, all of which she explores on her 1200+ article website, *TieDyeTravels.com*.

Robinson's journeys across Arkansas have earned her the title "road warrior," "traveling pie lady," and probably some minor epithets. Few have spent as much time exploring The Natural State, or researching its cuisine. "The Girl in the Hat" has been sighted in every one of Arkansas's 75 counties, oftentimes sliding behind a menu or peeking into a kitchen.

Kat lives with daughter Hunter and partner Grav Weldon in Little Rock.

You can contact the author at *kat@tiedyetravels.com* with questions or correspondence - or, of course, recommendations on great recipes and wonderful places to eat in Arkansas.

Books by Kat Robinson

Arkansas Pie:
A Delicious Slice of the Natural State
History Press, 2012

Classic Eateries of the Ozarks
and Arkansas River Valley
History Press, 2013

Classic Eateries of the Arkansas Delta
History Press, 2014

Another Slice of Arkansas Pie: A Guide to the
Best Restaurants, Bakeries, Truck Stops and Food
Trucks for Delectable Bites in The Natural State
Tonti Press, 2018

Arkansas Food:
The A to Z of Eating in The Natural State
Tonti Press, 2018

101 Things to Eat in Arkansas Before You Die
Tonti Press, 2019

102 More Things to Eat in Arkansas
Before You Die
Tonti Press, 2019

43 Tables:
An Internet Community Cooks During Quarantine
Tonti Press, 2020

A Bite of Arkansas:
A Cookbook of Natural State Delights
Tonti Press, 2020

Arkansas Dairy Bars: Neat Eats and Cool Treats
Tonti Press, 2021

and this book
Arkansas Cookery:
Retro Recipes from The Natural State
Tonti Press, 2021